The FOUR LAWS of LAWS

Guaranteed Success for Every Married Couple

LOVE

JIMMY EVANS

XO
PUBLISHING

XO
MARRIAGE®

The Four Laws of Love Study Guide
Copyright © 2024 by Jimmy Evans

ISBN: 978-1-960870-23-0

The companion book to this study guide is available in multiple formats:
ISBN: 978-1-950113-50-7 Paperback
ISBN: 978-1-950113-24-8 eBook
ISBN: 978-1-950113-25-5 Audiobook

XO Publishing is a leading creator of relationship-based resources. We focus primarily on marriage-related content for churches, small group curriculum, and people looking for timeless truths about relationships and overall marital health. For more information on other resources from XO Publishing, visit XOPublishing.com.

XO Marriage®, an imprint of XO Publishing
1021 Grace Lane
Southlake, Texas 76092

Printed in the United States of America
24 25 26 27—5 4 3 2 1

Table of Contents

Introduction

Welcome to *The Four Laws of Love Study Guide*! I created this study guide as a companion resource to *The Four Laws of Love*, and you will notice that it follows the same section and chapter order. The purpose of this study guide is to help you dive even deeper into the book's material so that you can incorporate the principles into your own life and marriage. You can use it for yourself, or better yet, read it together with your spouse. This study guide is also a helpful tool for leaders of small groups and marriage classes.

Here is the layout for each chapter in this study guide:

The Big Idea

This brief section presents the primary theme, thought, or truth from the chapter.

Review

The review summarizes the chapter's content and highlights important insights and details. It serves as a refresher if you have finished the chapter some days before you get to the discussion and reflection questions. The review can also be read aloud if you are going through the book with your spouse or with a small group or class.

Scripture Reading

I encourage you to read these Scriptures carefully and meditate on them throughout the day. What is the Holy Spirit saying to you through God's Word? Be sure to write down what you hear in your heart.

Discussion Questions

The discussion questions prompt you to recall important concepts and to think through particular applications. They are great conversation starters for couples, small groups, and classes. Individuals may find it helpful to write down their answers in a journal.

Reflection Questions

The reflection questions are more personal in nature and focus on your own relationship and experiences. They are best suited for personal and couple responses. This is another opportunity to journal your answers and let the Holy Spirit guide you in growing together. Even if you are doing this study guide alone, I encourage you to share your answers with your spouse. The best way to build your marriage is to build it *with* your spouse!

Connect with God

This sample prayer offers a conversation-starter with God about the things you have read and reflected on in the chapter. You can pray the prayer aloud by yourself, with your spouse, or with your group or class. But don't stop there! Ask the Holy Spirit to continue speaking to you and guiding you as you grow in your relationship with the Lord and with your spouse.

Leader Guide

Whether this is your first time to lead a small group, class, or book study or you have a lot of leadership experience, I am confident that God is going to use you in a powerful way. Lasting marriages are built on a foundation of love expressed through honesty, vulnerability, trust, and selflessness. You are partnering with God in providing opportunities for that to happen, and I am so thankful for you.

I've included a sample 60–minute session schedule to help you structure your time together. I've also listed some guidance on how to prepare for and lead these sessions. The best leader is, of course, the Holy Spirit. Always seek His guidance and listen to His direction. And if you need to make some adjustments, feel free to do so. The Holy Spirit's plan is always the best one!

Sample Session Schedule

Welcome: 5 minutes
Read ("Big Idea," "Review," and "Scripture Reading"): 20 minutes
Discussion Questions: 25 minutes
Prayer ("Connect with God"): 10 minutes

Before the Session

Pray

Prayer is the most important thing you can do to prepare. We all need God's help, and He is more than willing to come to our assistance if we will simply ask Him. Here are some prayer points to consider:

- Pray for each person's relationship with the Lord.
- Pray for each person's relationship with their spouse.
- Pray for each person's relationship with their children.
- Pray for the Holy Spirit to give you wisdom.

Prepare

Read the chapter in the book and in this study guide that you will be discussing in your next session. As you read, make notes of anything that stands out to you. These can be quotes from the text, Scripture passages, stories, ideas, and so forth. Next, review the discussion and personal reflection questions and mentally answer them for yourself. This will help you become more familiar with the material and build your confidence.

Plan Ahead

Assign a backup leader who will be prepared to lead the session if an emergency arises and you are unable to attend. Also, if you need to make a schedule change, do your best to communicate with everyone involved in advance. By keeping the lines of communication open, you build trust and cooperation.

During the Session

Be Punctual

Few things convey indifference as strongly as a leader who doesn't manage their time well. Yes, life can get in the way of the best intentions, but strive to arrive on time, or even early, for every session. Begin promptly and end on time. This demonstrates your respect for the time of everyone involved.

Be Engaged

The people in your small group, class, or book study will reflect your level of engagement. In other words, the more engaged you are, the more they will be too. Do your best to be 100 percent present and make a conscious effort to eliminate distractions. This includes turning off your cell phone or at least setting it on "silent" or "do not disturb" mode. Invite everyone else to do the same with their electronic devices.

Be Trustworthy

During the first session, set an expectation of safety and discretion. If the people in your small group, class, or book study don't already know each other, then it may take a little while for conversation to gain momentum. That's perfectly fine. Remember, you do not have to "teach" these chapters. Your responsibility is to set the stage for conversations, and the Holy Spirit will begin to move as people share their thoughts and feelings.

Be Compassionate

Every marriage experiences its share of ups and downs. Even if a couple chooses not to disclose any specifics, they may be facing their own challenges. There may be occasions when someone appears disengaged and reserved, or they might exhibit strong emotions during the conversation. These moments provide an opportunity to reflect the compassionate nature of our heavenly Father. As Psalm 86:15 states, "But you, O Lord, are a God of compassion and mercy, slow to get angry and filled with unfailing love and faithfulness." Allow the Holy Spirit to guide your words, actions, and demeanor, granting you wisdom in all your interactions.

Additionally, remember to extend compassion to yourself. There may be times when you feel inadequate or unprepared. Always bear in mind that there is only one perfect Leader: the King of kings and Lord of lords. Keep your focus on Jesus. As Proverbs 3:6 reminds us, "Seek his will in all you do, and he will show you which path to take."

Be Calm

When unexpected situations and dynamics arise, it's important for you as the leader to project a calm demeanor. Sometimes you may have individuals or couples who dominate the discussion or want to tell everyone what to do. In those situations, gently thank them for their input and invite others to speak. If necessary, feel free to talk with them outside of the session to ask them to help you create a hospitable environment that invites everyone to participate. Sometimes, simply asking someone for their help gives them a sense of responsibility, which can improve future sessions.

As you begin, I encourage you to remind yourself that the Lord will be alongside you every step of the way. You don't have to do this in your own strength. God will give you everything you need as you trust Him to lead through you.

1

The Law of Priority

THE BIG IDEA

Misplaced priorities are often the main culprit of failing marriages. God designed marriage to be the top priority in life after our relationship with Him. Any other arrangement leads to trouble.

REVIEW

In Genesis 2:24, God commands a man to leave his parents in order to "cleave" to his wife in marriage. In no way does this mean a man should abandon or abuse his parents. It simply means that the position of commitment and devotion that the parents once had in a man's life is relinquished and given instead to his wife. The parents are not given less honor; they are simply transferred to a lower-priority position.

The same instructions also apply to the wife. God designed marriage to be the husband and wife's top priority. Only our relationship with Him comes before that.

The reason so many marriages end in divorce is because of misplaced priorities. When other areas of life are placed before marriage, a spouse is bound to become jealous. While we tend to think of the sinful, destructive forms of jealousy, there is also *legitimate jealousy*. This type of jealousy is righteous. For example, if you witnessed someone trying to seduce your spouse, then you would become jealous—and rightly so! Legitimate jealousy is something God put in us in order to protect our marriages.

God Himself becomes jealous when we make other parts of our lives more important than Him. By devoting more time and energy to other people or activities, we make them our gods. In other words, we violate God's love for us. We are the bride of Christ (see Ephesians 5:22–33), and He loves us so passionately that He actively fights to protect our relationship with Him.

During the courtship days and the first few years of a marriage, couples put everything they have into their relationship and do all they can to protect it. Then, there is typically a decline in marital satisfaction with the arrival of children. Both spouses begin to prioritize other things (child-rearing, work, school, friends, hobbies, etc.) over their relationship. The more they see their spouse devote time to these other pursuits, the more they make themselves busy. It's a vicious cycle of feeling jealous and violated.

Time does not fix the problem. As the couple grows older, marital satisfaction gets lower. There may be a slight improvement after the children leave home, but it will still remain lower than when the marriage began. The longer we focus on the wrong priorities, the more destructive and self-defensive the relationship becomes.

But just because this is common does not mean that we all are doomed to live in a downward spiral! God designed marriage to get better as couples grow older together. As the years go by, we are meant to be more and more in love than we were in the beginning.

In every other area of life, the veterans always teach the rookies how to succeed. Yet when it comes to marriage, newly married couples tend to be the model of success because the veterans have more problems in their marriage. That's a little backwards, isn't it? It's time to fix the trend.

If we will obey God's command to prioritize our lives and keep our marriages higher than anything except our relationship with Him, marriage will work wonderfully. It *is* possible for marriage to work! It's just a matter of reordering priorities. Think about it. There's nothing satisfying about bringing a paycheck home to a broken marriage.

The benefits of the paycheck don't determine the marriage; it's the marriage that determines the benefits of the paycheck.

It is so important that our children are raised in a loving home that models marital harmony and a solid relationship with God. Then they will know how to have a successful marriage too. Even though it may sound counterintuitive, prioritizing your marriage over your children actually serves your children better in the long run.

Most priority lists should go something like this: God, spouse, children, church, extended family and close friends, career, and other interests (hobbies). If this is truly the order of our priorities, our lives will make it evident. It's easy to say that we love God, but if we give very little time and attention to Him, we reveal where we really stand. The same is true in marriage. In both cases, actions speak louder than words.

After setting your priorities, the biggest necessity (and challenge) will be to protect them from other demands that press in on you. Your time and energy are like money: they are limited assets that must be used wisely. God rightfully deserves the first and best of our time and energy, and your spouse deserves the second best. If any of your priorities receive little to nothing of your time and energy, let it be the ones at the bottom of the list.

God's design for marriage is perfect. If you feel something is off in your marriage in terms of priority, it is best to act right away and fix the problems before they get out of hand. The results will be something awesome and beautiful.

SCRIPTURE READING

Therefore a man shall leave his father and mother and be joined to his wife, and they shall become one flesh (Genesis 2:24).

"Do not worship any other god, for the LORD, whose name is Jealous, is a jealous God" (Exodus 34:14 NIV).

"But seek first the kingdom of God and His righteousness, and all these things shall be added to you" (Matthew 6:33).

DISCUSSION QUESTIONS

1. Does the saying, "The honeymoon is over" reflect how God designed marriage to function over time? Why or why not?

2. What role does legitimate jealousy play in protecting the priority of marriage?

3. How can priorities be protected during different seasons of life, such as having a new baby, raising kids, losing a job, etc.?

4. How can couples encourage each other instead of getting frustrated or jealous about misplaced priorities?

5. What boundaries need to be set with children in order to keep marriage a priority? What boundaries need to be set with extended family members?

REFLECTION QUESTIONS

1. Do you think couples today feel pressure to put their children, careers, and other priorities before their marriage? If yes, where does this pressure come from?

2. How does the idea that time and energy must be budgeted change how you approach your priorities?

3. Are there activities or people whom you prioritize over God? After God, have you put anything above your spouse?

4. How would making your marriage your top priority benefit your children?

5. What are your most important priorities? How can you protect them?

CONNECT WITH GOD

Dear Father, You designed marriage to reflect Your love for the Church. Please forgive us for the times we have failed to keep You as our first priority and our spouse as the second priority. We repent, Lord, and we commit to protecting our priorities with both our words and our actions. Guard our marriages from distractions and intrusions. Transform our hearts and teach us to be the spouses You designed us to be. In Jesus' name, Amen.

2

Prioritized Communication

THE BIG IDEA

Communication requires time, effort, and consistency. Done the right way, it can transform a marriage and lead to greater intimacy and partnership in the relationship.

REVIEW

The cornerstone of your commitment to putting your marriage above every other human relationship or pursuit is prioritized communication. You can't microwave communication, and there's no substitute for it. If you're too busy to talk, then you need to find another area of your life to sacrifice rather than sacrificing your marriage. There's no way you can obey the law of priority and not communicate with your spouse in a way that meets their needs. Husbands must understand that open and honest communication isn't just a "want" for women—it's one of their deepest needs.

Committing to communicate regularly with your spouse will bring your marriage back on track and create deeper intimacy, both emotionally and sexually. But in order to communicate, you need to have skills and understanding to keep you from getting stuck or frustrated.

Five Pillars of Communication

1. Tone

The tone you use makes all the difference in the world. You can say the same thing in two different tones and convey two completely different things. The tone you use immediately gives away whether or not you care.

Our tones should always communicate respect, care, and value. At the same time, husbands and wives need to be understanding of one another because men and women have different needs and sensitivities. A woman needs to know that she can find security in her husband, that he values her, and that he will meet her needs with selflessness and sensitivity. A man needs to know that his wife is proud of him and that she respects him.

2. Time

Communication requires consistency. Proactive communication means sitting down before events happen, praying it through, and making a plan. Without a plan, life becomes more difficult, and tensions build. Personal communication is everyday conversation that is crucial in order to connect and share personal issues without any distractions. It is important to set aside time to process our thoughts and emotions so that our relationship can stay healthy. Intimate communication should also be daily. This is communication that is loving, encouraging, praising, affectionate, and sometimes even sexual. It also keeps negativity and criticism out of your marriage.

3. Trust

The deeper the level of communication, the more trust is built. To build trust, we have to make ourselves vulnerable and expose our hearts, even at the risk of hurt, betrayal, or rejection. Remember, *trust is earned in drops and lost in buckets*. Years of trust can be shattered in a very short time. If you have violated your spouse's trust, you can begin to earn it back by sincerely apologizing and taking responsibility for your mistakes.

4. Truth

Truth and love must always go together. Truth without love is mean, and love without truth is meaningless. But truth in love creates meaningful communication. The Bible is the ultimate standard of truth, and we must also be able to openly share "our truth"—our feelings. Our feelings are very real, even though they aren't always right, and it is important to have the freedom in marriage to be open about them without being attacked or accused. Sometimes we need the ability to complain (but never criticize) about a situation in order to get our feelings off our chest. This creates an atmosphere of honesty rather than one of defensiveness and hostility. In order to succeed, a husband and wife need to be willing to hear where they can improve so that they can better understand each other's needs. And they need to remain aware of the small issues that may pile up and turn into a much bigger problem.

5. Teamwork

God create men and women with intentional differences. The surest way to make a marriage fail is to try to change those differences. The four basic needs of a woman are security, open and honest communication, soft and nonsexual affection, and leadership. The four basic needs of a man are honor, sex, friendship with his wife, and domestic support. Compatibility in marriage isn't based on sameness. It's based on shared faith, character, values, and life goals. Solid communication involves letting our spouse know that we accept and celebrate their differences.

SCRIPTURE READING

A soft answer turns away wrath,
But a harsh word stirs up anger (Proverbs 15:1).

Speaking the truth in love, [we] may grow up in all things into Him who is the head—Christ (Ephesians 4:15).

Therefore be imitators of God as dear children. And walk in love, as Christ also has loved us and given Himself for us, an offering and a sacrifice to God for a sweet-smelling aroma (Ephesians 5:1–2).

DISCUSSION QUESTIONS

1. Why is communication often a struggle in marriages? What makes it difficult?
2. What are some practical ways couples can set aside undistracted time for regular communication based on their needs and schedules? What sort of sacrifices might have to be made?
3. How can trust be lost in a marriage? What are keys to rebuilding trust?
4. How can unresolved minor issues threaten intimacy over time?

5. Why is it important to accept and celebrate our spouse's differences instead of trying to change them to be like us?

REFLECTION QUESTIONS

1. What feelings or past experiences make communicate a challenge in your marriage? How can you address any barriers?

2. Why do you think open communication and emotional intimacy often lead to increased physical intimacy as well?

3. What are some ways you can convey security, love, and respect in your tone when communicating with your spouse, even during disagreements?

4. Which of your spouse's differences have been hardest for you to accept? How can you celebrate those differences more going forward?

5. Which of the Five Pillars of Communication is the most challenging for you currently? How can you grow in that area?

CONNECT WITH GOD

Dear Father, communication can be very difficult sometimes. Work in us so that we can be better communicators with our spouses. Help us not to bottle things up but to address issues promptly. We want to be better spouses, Lord, and we know it will take hard work and consistency. May we always respond in love as we strive to be understanding of our spouses' feelings and differences. Let the words of our mouths and the thoughts of our hearts be pleasing to You. In Jesus' name, Amen.

3

Prioritized Relationships

THE BIG IDEA

The greatest threat to most marriages is from good things out of priority. Most often, it is from relationships with family or friends that intrude upon the priority of the marriage and create legitimate jealousy in one or both spouses.

REVIEW

For your marriage to succeed, you must prioritize your relationship with your spouse over every other relationship in your life, except for your relationship with Jesus. When you allow your friends or family to intrude on your marriage, you stir up legitimate jealousy in your spouse.

Prioritizing your spouse over everyone else will sometimes be very difficult, and it might even make some people angry. But protecting your marriage is worth it.

The most common relationship that compromises marriages is with your children. Children want unlimited access to their parents and will not naturally respect the boundaries of your marriage unless they are taught. The worst thing for parents to do is to try to be "super-parents" (or "helicopter parents") because all of their energy is put into hovering over their children. They never leave any time to be with each other.

Children are an important assignment from God. But they are also a temporary assignment. One day they will grow up and leave our homes to start their own lives and families. Our marriages, on the other hand, are permanent—or at least they should be. Just like our children don't appreciate us breathing down their necks at all times, we should not allow them to get away with the same.

When children become the center of their parents' universe, the law of priority is broken, and over the years resentment begins to grow between husband and wife. But it's never too late to do the right thing. If your children have become your top priority, first repent and ask forgiveness from your spouse. From then on, stop responding to the constant demands of your children. Love and care for them, but teach them to respect the boundaries of your marriage.

Create new disciplines in your marriage to redirect your time and energy to your spouse in a prioritized, regular manner. This may seem difficult if the passion has faded from your relationship, but don't let your feelings dictate your words and actions. When you consistently do the right thing, the passion will return.

Disciplines and traditions are crucial for a marriage. It doesn't matter what you can make happen once; rather, it matters what you can keep happening. Some examples of good disciplines and traditions include a weekly date night, praying together and going to church, taking walks together, planning times to have sex when you are both rested, talking face-to-face daily with no distractions, and finding something you both enjoy doing and doing it regularly.

Relationships with the in-laws can also create problems for married couples. God designed marriage to be a cleaving of a man and a woman. In the process, they both *leave* their parents, which is a reprioritization of their affections.

But sometimes parents don't want to let go, or perhaps one or both spouses don't want to let go of their parents. Maybe the parents are trying to control their child in some way, or they become adversarial towards their child's spouse. In any of these cases, the solution is to maintain the law of priority, giving priority to one's spouse over one's parents. The parents that consider their child as the center of their universe are problem in-laws in training. From the start, your relationship with your spouse must be carefully protected and preserved. Otherwise, resentment and hostility will begin to develop.

Of course, honor should still be given to the parents, but honor and authority should not be confused. The moment we leave our parents to cleave to our spouses, we are responsible for making our own decisions, and our parents do not have the authority to change those decisions. The one caveat here is if you are still taking money from your parents. In that case, they deserve to have a louder voice in your life, as long as they do not violate the law of priority. But if tensions arise, especially between the in-laws and the non-biological spouse, it is the responsibility of the biological spouse to correct the issue. Resist any attempts at or threats of manipulation. Stand your ground lovingly, no matter what is said.

Friends should also be lower in priority. If you consider them more important than your spouse, it will only lead to jealousy and trouble. There are even some friends that we have to let go of after we're married. If they are ungodly, unhealthy, or don't respect the boundaries of your marriage, they need to be removed for the sake of your relationship with your spouse.

Another issue in these modern times is our use of technology and social media. Because of technology, we are rarely alone, and it can easily distract us from our relationship with our spouse. In fact, too many divorces happen because of technology and social media. If you can't put down your devices for some quality time, you are in bondage to that device.

Marriage is the most important human relationship we will ever have, and it is worth protecting, no matter the cost. When we make those sacrifices, we show our spouse that we clearly love them. That will lead to a long and happy future!

SCRIPTURE READING

Therefore shall a man leave his father and his mother, and shall cleave unto his wife (Genesis 2:24 KJV).

See then that you walk circumspectly, not as fools but as wise, redeeming the time, because the days are evil (Ephesians 5:15–16).

To everything *there is* a season,
> A time for every purpose under heaven (Ecclesiastes 3:1).

DISCUSSION QUESTIONS

1. How can children impact the priority of a marriage that lacks proper boundaries? What are some ways to set and enforce boundaries?

2. What are some important daily or weekly disciplines couples should practice in order to increase their intimacy?

3. What does the concept of "leaving and cleaving" mean for setting proper priorities in marriage? Why is this important?

4. How can friends negatively impact a marriage? When is it best to end such friendships?

5. How can technology and social media interfere with marriage priorities? What rules can couples implement?

REFLECTION QUESTIONS

1. What should you do if your parents try to control you financially or otherwise after marriage? How can you lovingly address this?

2. Do you have any friendships that your spouse feels threatened by? Why might that be and how can you respond?

3. Could technology or social media be distracting you from your spouse? What boundaries can you put in place?

4. How often do you and your spouse pray together? How can you grow in your spiritual intimacy?

5. What are the greatest threats to the priority of your marriage right now? How can you address them?

CONNECT WITH GOD

Dear Father, thank You for the gift of marriage and for teaching us how to honor it through Your Word. As we fix our eyes on You, show us see what relationships we have been prioritizing over You and over our spouses. Help us to create boundaries around our marriages with firm but gentle love and strengthen us when we need to enforce those boundaries. Please forgive us for any distractions I have allowed to creep in. May our marriages reflect Your love and glory. In Jesus' name, Amen.

4

Prioritized Romance

THE BIG IDEA

Romance is not meant to be a seasonal fad. It must be a prioritized, prominent feature in your marriage relationship if you are going to keep your passion and intimacy alive and growing.

REVIEW

The sinful, fallen world around us teaches that marriage is a miserable state of being that can go nowhere but downhill after the honeymoon is over. But that is not God's desire for us. He created marriage to be filled with romance so that the husband and wife could grow in their love for one another as the years go by. Even if a relationship has grown stale, it can be revived.

According to the laws of physics, all matter is either dynamic, static, or entropic. In other words, it's either growing, has just stopped growing, or is dying. Therefore, if something (such as a relationship) is not continuously growing, it will become static, and it'll only get worse from there. Thankfully, in Christ, all things become new. With His help and some practical steps, the passions that died can be restored.

Four Elements of Romance

1. Meeting an unspoken need or desire in your spouse

Romantic love is special because it anticipates the needs and desires of the spouse and immediately acts on them. This means doing something for them before they even ask you. How powerful that is! By doing something special for your spouse, you demonstrate that you care about them and that you're thinking about them even when you could be focused on other things.

When we first fall in love, our affections grow stronger and more electrifying because we are actively trying to please our prospective spouse. But after we're married, that electricity tends to fizzle out because we get lazy and stop doing those extra little things for each other. We stop studying each other and learning each other's likes and dislikes. In short, we stop romancing each other.

But Jesus told the church of Ephesus to return to Him, their "first love" (see Revelation 2:4–5). That must mean that it is possible for us to do the same in marriage. And it is! We can fan the flame by doing what we once did: paying attention to our spouse's needs and desires. It doesn't matter if you feel like doing it or not. You don't even have to feel in love. Just doing it will bring back those lost emotions.

We fall in love for two reasons: there are admirable qualities in the other person, and we like the way they makes us feel about ourselves. We pay attention to them, and they pay attention to us. Romantic love grows out of this. And if it could create romance once, it can do it again. It won't revive overnight, but if you remain committed and consistent, that love will grow.

2. Speaking love in your spouse's language

No matter what anybody says, both men and women need romance. They just need it in different ways. In marriage, women need security, open and honest communication, soft and nonsexual affection, and leadership. Men need honor (respect), sex, friendship with their wife, and domestic support. Women tend to see romance as emotionally connected, conversational, mostly nonsexual, and male initiated. Men see romance as honoring, sexual, fun, and comfortable.

The trouble starts when one or both spouses don't accept their partner's needs as being legitimate. Usually this is because the spouse's needs are so different that it's hard to understand why it is a need at all. That's the surest way to kill a relationship. A marriage must be a win-win proposition, which means that your spouse's needs are just as important as your own. Both of you should work consistently to meet each other's needs. This includes accepting and honoring your differences and pursuing each other with full force.

Just as it's important to be aware of your spouse's needs and desires, you also need to be aware of their love language. Do they like to cuddle? Do they like it when you talk with them privately? Selflessness in marriage is critical to seeing the relationship succeed, especially when that selflessness is mutual.

3. Communicating unique value to your spouse

Romance is the private, intimate side of a marriage. It is only meant for one person. If you show romantic love or do romantic things for other people, then it doesn't mean a thing to your spouse when you try to be romantic with them. Romantic love communicates that your spouse is special, unique, and highly valued. It's how we prioritize marriage over all other relationships. Otherwise, there wouldn't be any difference at all, apart from having sex.

4. Empathy

Empathy is the ability to understand and share the feelings of another person. We have natural empathy when we are dating because we want to show the other person that we truly care for them and what they are feeling. When we know that we are heard and cared for, it creates a safe and sensitive environment that cultivates romantic love. But when we stop showing empathy in marriage, we begin to feel unsafe where we used to feel comfortable.

There are 12 phases of romantic love:

1. Awareness
2. Interest
3. Positive exchange
4. Romantic interest
5. High emotional focus
6. Positive romantic exchange
7. Strong feelings of love and passion
8. Deepening relational bonds
9. Normalcy (routine, lack of novelty)
10. Reality (conflict, difficulty, fatigue, illness)
11. Distraction and disinterest
12. Loss of romance

The phase "high emotional focus" is the empathy that is always present in romantic love. Even after that phase, passions can escalate. But when we begin to show less empathy, we fall into "normalcy" and "reality," and the romance fades.

Romance isn't complicated or difficult. But it does require intentionality and proactivity. Through romance, we show that we truly do prioritize our marriage.

SCRIPTURE READING

"To the angel of the church of Ephesus write,

'These things says He who holds the seven stars in His right hand, who walks in the midst of the seven golden lampstands: "I know your works, your labor, your patience, and that you cannot bear those who are evil. And you have tested those who say they are apostles and are not, and have found them liars; and you have persevered and have patience, and have labored for My name's sake and have not become weary. Nevertheless I have *this* against you, that you have left your first love. Remember therefore from where you have fallen; repent and do the first works, or else I will come to you quickly and remove your lampstand from its place—unless you repent"'" (Revelation 2:1–5).

Therefore, if anyone *is* in Christ, *he is* a new creation; old things have passed away; behold, all things have become new (2 Corinthians 5:17).

DISCUSSION QUESTIONS

1. How do the laws of physics also govern relationships? How might understanding this help married couples?

2. What are some examples of romance "killers" that stem from spouses not accepting one another's needs?

3. Romance tends to fade when couples stop doing the things that made the relationship good in the beginning. What are some of the things that fade in most marriages? How can spouses recapture them?

4. Why is it important that a spouse's romantic expression communicates unique value to their partner? What happens when romantic expressions are generic?

5. Why is it so hard for spouses to enthusiastically meet a need they personally don't share? How can empathy be strengthened in these situations?

REFLECTION QUESTIONS

1. Reflect on your spouse's unspoken preferences and desires. What are some little things you can do without being asked to show them your love?

2. What do you think of the list of four major needs of men and women in marriage? Do you agree or disagree with these distinctions? What needs resonate with you most?

3. What do you say and do on a consistent basis that communicates unique value to your spouse?

4. Have busyness, fatigue, or familiarity dulled the romance in your marriage? How can this be counteracted and the romance be revived?

5. Which ideas from this chapter do you think will be most helpful for improving romance in your marriage? Why?

CONNECT WITH GOD

Dear Father, help us to return to our first love with You and with our spouses. We repent for the times we have selfishly put our own needs and desires above those of our spouses. Help us to learn what our spouses need and how they feel most loved. Most of all, soften our hearts so that we may feel empathy towards them and value them as the gifts that they are. Let the passion return and may our marriages get better and better. In Jesus' name, Amen.

5

The Law of Pursuit

THE BIG IDEA

There may be times in marriage when the love you once had for one another seems lost for good. In those moments, you must actively pursue and cling to your spouse as God commanded and trust that with the Lord's help and hard work, that romantic edge can be restored.

REVIEW

"I just don't love him anymore." "I made a mistake when I married her." Disillusionment is a very real experience that can lead to both spouses saying terrible things to one another and hurting each other. Be encouraged that there is a remedy!

In Genesis 2:24, after God commands us to leave (relinquish or loosen the bonds of) our parents, He says we are to *cleave* to our spouse. There are two definitions to the word "cleave" in the English language. The first is to separate or to chop into two pieces. But it is the second definition that is being used in this verse: "to pursue with great energy" and "to zealously cling to something." That is what God wants us to do when we marry—to zealously pursue each other and cling to each other for the rest of our lives. Love in marriage doesn't "just happen." Marriage takes work in order to succeed.

Think back to when you first began dating your spouse. You were willing to do almost anything to impress them! Your relationship didn't "just happen" because of perfect chemistry. It involved a lot of hard work. And once you stop working hard to care for your spouse, your relationship will inevitably take a downhill turn.

Marriage is like a muscle in our bodies: the more you work at it, the stronger and more attractive it will become. But if you stop working at it, it will become weak and unattractive. The longer you don't work at it, the less you'll feel like doing it. Starting back up again can be hard and even painful, but your spouse is worth the work. Besides, it's much easier to work hard at the relationship you're in now than to divorce, spiff yourself up in order to remarry, and experience the same decline all over again. The only way to get rid of a problem for good is to face it head-on and solve it.

Maybe someone is already in an affair and feels loved for the first time in a long time. They may believe they could never be satisfied with their spouse again. But affairs are always wrong in God's sight, and they are always destructive no matter how good they may seem. Hear that again: Affairs are never of God! They are shaky ground because you can never know for certain that the person won't leave you too once the going gets tough.

No matter how bad your marriage may seem right now, if you are willing to work hard at loving your spouse, then you will begin to see a difference in your marriage. Above all, you can choose to see your spouse as the right person for you rather than dreaming about your ideal spouse. This will help increase the joy in your marriage.

Three Steps to Heal and Revive Love

Maybe your marriage needs to be healed and restored. In Revelation 2:5, Jesus gives the Ephesian Christians three steps to revive their love for Him. With the help of the Holy Spirit, these same three steps will heal and revive the love of any couple.

1. Remember therefore from where you have fallen.

When you first became a Christian, you were willing do to almost anything for God. But over time, if you allow other things to steal your attention from Him, you will lose your first love for Him.

Love is a decision of the will; it cannot be based on emotions. To return to our first love, we must commit to acting in another's best interest regardless of how we feel. This goes for our relationship with God and with our spouse. When we first loved our spouses, we did everything we could for them and were excited to do it. We honored them with our words and actions.

2. *Repent.*

In the Bible, the word *repent* means "to change your mind" or "to turn around." When you first dated your spouse, you were going in the right direction. You treated them right and showed them that you loved them. But at some point, you began going in the wrong direction, and you lost the first love you once had for your spouse. How do you fix this? You turn around and go in the right direction again!

When you complete step one, you receive the revelation that what you were once doing right you are now doing wrong. The next step, then, is to turn around. True repentance includes acknowledging the truth (revelation), admitting you were wrong (confession), and adjusting your direction (action).

3. Do the deeds you did at first.

Having changed course, you can now begin doing what you did when you first fell in love. The most important thing to know about this step is that emotions are not required. We can't work up emotions, and Jesus never demands us to do so anyway. Emotions come naturally after we take the time and energy to pursue God and our spouse.

If your love turned cold some time ago, it can be difficult and even embarrassing to become emotionally vulnerable again. Love is an act of faith. You will still experience hardships at times in your marriage, but God is faithful, and He will honor even your weakest moments of faith. The more you step out in faith and return to how your marriage was at the beginning, the more addicted you will become to that labor of love!

SCRIPTURE READING

And shall cleave unto his wife (Genesis 2:24 KJV)

In all labor there is profit,
But idle chatter *leads* only to poverty
(Proverbs 14:23).

Remember therefore from where you have fallen; repent and do the first works, or else I will come to you quickly and remove your lampstand from its place—unless you repent (Revelation 2:5).

DISCUSSION QUESTIONS

1. How can remembering the past help give us the right perspective to fix current marital struggles?

2. What does it mean to "cleave" to one's spouse? What are some tangible ways to do that daily?

3. Why do emotions and feelings make an unstable foundation for love and relationships?

4. If both spouses commit to meeting each other's needs daily, how might that positively impact challenges like financial strain or parenting disagreements?

5. What role does faith play in motivating spouses to pursue renewal? How so?

REFLECTION QUESTIONS

1. In what ways have Hollywood's depictions of romance shaped your views of love and marriage? How might these ideas be harmful to your marriage?

2. What were some of the sweet, joyful details from the beginning of your relationship with your spouse? What could you do to recapture that energy?

3. What attitudes or behaviors might you need to repent of and change to restore intimacy in your marriage?

4. What fears, hesitations, or obstacles arise in you when you consider repenting and restoring romance in your marriage? How can these be overcome?

5. What is one practical thing you can do this week to actively cleave to and cherish your spouse?

CONNECT WITH GOD

Dear Father, we need Your wisdom and guidance. Show us how to pursue our spouses with energy, sensitivity, and diligence. When our feelings are lacking, help us to remember our first love, repent of wrong attitudes, and do the deeds we did at first. Give us strength to obey Your commands, even when our emotions tempt us not to. Renew our passion for our spouses and fill our hearts with Your love. In Jesus' name, Amen.

6

God's Perfect Plan for Marriage

THE BIG IDEA

In God's perfect design for marriage that He gives us in His Word, husbands and wives have unique roles. A husband is to love and sacrifice for his wife, and a wife is to respect her husband. Following these roles allows us to have the intimacy and partnership God intends for us to have.

REVIEW

As we work to pursue our spouses, it is important that our work is in alignment with God's design for marriage. God created husbands and wives to be equals, but He also gave them their own roles within their marriage. This design is found in Ephesians 5.

Now, many Christians don't like this passage. More specifically, they like what is says about their spouses but not what it says about themselves. They also fear being the first one to follow God's design because it could leave them vulnerable if their spouse refuses to change in response. Both husbands and wives fear that their spouse will run right over them if they are the only ones to follow God's plan. But there is no alternative. This is the only plan God has revealed, and nothing we can come up with will ever be better.

Women often reject Ephesians 5:22–24 because it has been used out of context to tell them to submit to their husbands no matter what. This has created a lot of pain and resentment. But the verse that comes before creates the context: "Submitting to one another in the fear of God" (Ephesians 5:21). Both wives *and* husbands should submit to each other. After that, the apostle Paul devotes three verses to telling the wives how to do so and *five* verses to telling the husbands how to do so.

God's plan for marriage is not for the husband to dominate his wife. Instead, He created marriage to be shared between two equals who are both submitted to God and each other with a servant-like mindset.

Jesus Christ is the perfect Lord because He is a loving, gentle, and humble servant-leader. Those qualities draw us to Him. Those same qualities are meant to be found in a Christian husband, especially in the way he treats and leads his wife. A husband submits to God and his wife by sacrificially loving her and caring for her as his equal. The wife submits to God and her husband by honoring him as she would the Lord Himself. The most important thing to remember is that neither the husband nor the wife is the boss. Jesus is the one who is meant to be in charge. Through this plan, both spouses' needs are met, and the marriage is a win-win.

God's plan for marriage is absolutely perfect, and here are three reasons why:

God's plan makes us attractive to our spouses.

According to Ephesians 5, husbands are meant to be sacrificial servant-leaders for their wives, nourishing and cherishing them as they would their own bodies. Women are more attracted to a man's care and character than to his physique or "manliness." According to research, wives find their husbands more attractive when they are doing housework, and husbands who share in the housework and childcare duties have more sex than those who don't.

Wives are meant to respect their husbands as they would Christ Himself. Now, they are still completely equal with their husbands—they simply have a different role. Men are more attracted to a woman's inner disposition of respect and loyalty than they are to outer beauty. So you see, God assigned men and women roles that make them more attractive to each other.

God's plan releases the potential in both husbands and wives.

According to Ephesians 5:29, men are to "nourish and cherish" their wives as Christ does the Church. By nourishing (feeding to maturity) and cherishing (keeping warm) their wives, husbands partner with God to bring their wives to their full potential and protect them from the world's perspective that they are only a sex object.

Women can help their husbands reach their full potential by providing the positive environment of respect that he needs and being a good cheerleader. This even means knowing how to say negative things in a positive way. Men flourish most in an atmosphere of praise, encouragement, and positive support, while demeaning words and actions make them wither.

God's plan neutralizes our sin natures and keeps them from damaging our marriages.

The reason we don't like what Ephesians 5 says about us is because our sin natures don't like it. That passage asks us to behave in a godly, selfless manner and leaves no room for us to be selfish. Unfortunately, being selfish is what comes naturally.

In the Garden of Eden, Adam and Eve both sinned by eating the forbidden fruit. As a result, we have inherited their sin natures. When they sinned, they sinned in different ways. Adam was told directly by God that he was not to eat the forbidden fruit. When the serpent began to tempt Eve, Adam remained silent and passive when he should have taken action to obey God and protect his wife. But he didn't. Today, when marriage problems arise, most men ignore them and become passive towards their wives.

When the serpent seduced Eve, she never consulted Adam who was standing right there with her, and she didn't consult God with whom she and Adam talked regularly. Today, wives tend to become stubbornly defiant over marital issues and refuse to receive input from God or their husbands. That is why Paul directs wives to submit to their husbands as they would to Christ.

SCRIPTURE READING

Submitting to one another in the fear of God.

Wives, submit to your own husbands as to the Lord. For the husband is head of the wife, as also Christ is head of the church; and He is the Savior of the body. Therefore, just as the church is subject to Christ, so *let* the wives *be* to their own husbands in everything.

Husbands, love your wives, just as Christ also loved the church and gave Himself for her, that He might sanctify and cleanse her with the washing of water by the word, that He might present her to Himself a glorious church, not having spot or wrinkle or any such thing, but that she should be holy and without blemish. So husbands ought to love their own wives as their own bodies; he who loves his wife loves himself. For no one ever hated his own flesh, but nourishes and cherishes it, just as the Lord *does* the church. For we are members of His body, of His flesh and of His bones. "For this reason a man shall leave his father and mother and be joined to his wife, and the two shall become one flesh." This is a great mystery, but I speak concerning Christ and the church. Nevertheless let each one of you in particular so love his own wife as himself, and let the wife *see* that she respects *her* husband (Ephesians 5:21–33).

DISCUSSION QUESTIONS

1. Why is it often difficult for spouses to accept what Ephesians 5 says about their own role? What causes this resistance?

2. What model of leadership does Paul give to husbands? How is this different from worldly perspectives on marriage?

3. Why is mutual submission in marriage a win-win proposition? What needs are met for both husbands and wives?

4. What inner quality is most important for wives to cultivate? Why is this attractive to husbands?

5. How do the sin natures of men and women differ? How do the roles found in Ephesians 5 counteract these?

REFLECTION QUESTIONS

1. Are you nurturing an environment where your spouse can blossom into who God made them to be? What could you do to help them reach their full potential?

2. What behaviors most clearly communicate honor and respect for your spouse?

3. Do you see mutual submission in marriage as a win-win? How could embracing this perspective strengthen your marriage?

4. Have you ignored issues in your marriage that hurt your relationship with your spouse? How can these issues ben addressed?

5. Are you zealously pursuing your spouse, or are you expecting them to change first? How can you take the first steps to pursue them?

CONNECT WITH GOD

Dear Father, thank You that Your plans are always perfect. You made no mistake when You designed marriage. I am so grateful that You gave me my spouse so that we could work as a team for Your glory. Teach me how to honor my spouse as I honor You. I want to help my spouse reach their full potential in Christ. In Jesus' name, Amen.

7

The Servant Rules

THE BIG IDEA

For a marriage to work, husbands and wives must have a servant spirit, making the other's needs a priority and serving joyfully by grace even when they don't deserve it.

REVIEW

Marriage only works when you work at it. What you do depends on what you want to accomplish. But what are we working to accomplish in marriage? We are working to meet our spouse's needs, even though they are probably very different than our own needs. Since we don't always understand why our spouse has those needs, a marriage is most successful when both spouses have a servant spirit.

Every husband has what his wife needs. And every wife has what her husband needs. Marriage is a joy when both the husband and the wife open their hearts and lives to serve each other. A selfish nature that always expects to receive without giving will erode a marriage.

Servant Rules

Serve what your spouse needs in spite of what you need, want, or understand.
Again, men and women have different needs within marriage. Women need security, open and honest communication, soft and nonsexual affection, and leadership. Men need honor (respect), sex, friendship with their wife, and domestic support. These needs may vary slightly from person to person, but overall, they are generally true.

Marriage is the most satisfying when spouses work to meet each other's (sinless) needs without judgment whether they understand them or not. Only you can meet your spouse's needs, just as only they can meet your needs.

Enjoy serving your spouse and do it with a joyful attitude.
If we only see our spouse as someone who is there to serve us and get us to where we want to go in our lives, our marriages will be miserable. Serving is a joy, and it becomes more of a joy the more we do it, especially when we do it without expecting to receive anything in return. Serving our spouses with a joyful attitude communicates love, acceptance,

value, and priority to them. This changes a marriage from an unemotional relationship to one filled with intimacy.

Reject score keeping and do what you do with a spirit of grace and faith.

Serving someone when things are going well is one thing. It's a whole other story when things get tough. The reason behind why we serve each other is revealed in these times. It is either from the Holy Spirit creating Christlikeness within us or because we expect something in return as a reward for our good behavior.

It's common in marriage to expect a give-and-take when it comes to serving each other. But when you expect something in return for your servant behavior, you create a self-protecting punishment and reward program based on your performance and on your spouse's performance. No one can live up to that! Serving must be purely an act of grace, untouched by our emotions and circumstances. It's very easy to fight anger with anger, or resentment with resentment, but it only makes a relationship more destructive. The hard thing to do is to fight anger with love and resentment with kindness. But it is Christ's nature to fight a negative spirit with the exact opposite spirit.

Vigilantly protect the time and energy necessary to serve your spouse.

Whom we spend the most time with and do the most for reveals who is our priority. God should always be our number one priority. After that should come our spouse. To protect our marriages, we must be disciplined and dedicated to preserving our time and energy for our spouse.

Expect to be blessed and don't get discouraged and give up.

Above all, when working at your relationship, you must realize that you will not always see the results you want, even when you're doing the right thing. In those times, you may think that nothing will ever change, and you'll be tempted to just give up. You may not see your spouse change in a day (or even in a month). Loving them can be quite the challenge, but when you feel most discouraged, look to Jesus. He promises that when we give undeserved love and kindness, He will cause His grace to abound to us in return. You're racking up blessings from heaven, and in the process, you're ministering well to someone who desperately needs it.

SCRIPTURE READING

"Whoever desires to become great among you, let him be your servant" (Matthew 20:26).

"But I say to you who hear: Love your enemies, do good to those who hate you, bless those who curse you, and pray for those who spitefully use you. To him who strikes you on the *one* cheek, offer the other also. And from him who takes away your cloak, do not withhold *your* tunic either. Give to everyone who asks of you. And from him who takes away your goods do not ask *them* back. And just as you want men to do to you, you also do to them likewise" (Luke 6:27–31).

"But love your enemies, do good, and lend, hoping for nothing in return; and your reward will be great, and you will be sons of the Most High. For He is kind to the unthankful and evil. Therefore be merciful, just as your Father also is merciful" (Luke 6:35–36).

DISCUSSION QUESTIONS

1. Do you agree with the four basic needs outlined for women and men? Would you add or change any? Why?

2. Why is it important to emphasize serving with joy rather than obligation? How can this be done?

3. What prevents couples from listening to and serving their spouse's needs? How can these obstacles be overcome?

4. How can focusing on biblical promises for serving help couples persevere through resistance from a spouse?

5. Which servant attitude do you think might come most unnaturally to people and require even more dependence on the Holy Spirit?

REFLECTION QUESTIONS

1. Do unmet needs cause frustration or problems in your marriage? How can you work through it?

2. Has serving your spouse without immediate results ever tempted you to give up? How can you persist?

3. How can you be more intentional about protecting your time and energy for your marriage?

4. In what ways can working to understand your spouse's needs cultivate a servant spirit?

5. How could the Servant Rules transform expectations and assumptions about roles in your marriage?

CONNECT WITH GOD

Dear Father, I want to learn to be a servant to You and to my spouse. Would You please teach me today? Help me to put aside my own wants so that I can serve my spouse without any expectation of receiving something in return. You are the ultimately Provider of my needs, and You are gracious to meet my heart's desires. Help me not to depend on my spouse but to depend entirely on You. In Jesus' name, Amen.

8

Married on Purpose

THE BIG IDEA

God put you with your spouse for a reason. If you don't know the reason, take time together to seek God. Place every area of your relationship under Him and ask Him for the vision He has for you!

REVIEW

Christian couples tend to realize that God put them together, but they don't always know why. Learning this "why" is sure to take your relationship to a deeper level. Couples also don't always know how to raise up each child so that they fulfill God's specific plan for their lives. They don't know what God's will is for each individual child. It is our duty as spouses and parents to seek God's will and receive His vision for our marriages and our children.

A vision retreat with your spouse doesn't have to be an expensive trip. It's simply a time to get away together where you can surrender every part of your marriage to the Lord and write down what He reveals to you. You'll be surprised at how this alone time will bring greater unity and strength to your marriage. Couples often fight because they have different visions for their life together. With a unified vision, there is peace.

Five Virtues of Vision

1. Clarity

How do you know you're succeeding if you don't know what you're trying to accomplish? Without knowing God's vision, you're building a house without blueprints. We have been put with our spouses for a specific purpose, not just to go through the motions of marriage.

2. Energy

When you capture the vision and gain clarity, you become invigorated and motivated in your marriage. The Lord told Habakkuk to write down the vision He would give him so that those who read it may *run* (see Habakkuk 2:2). When you have no vision (when you're blind), you can't run. You could easily bump into something or trip and injure yourself. You don't know where you're going. God gives us vision so that we can clearly understand His will and energetically pursue it.

3. Purity

When we have no clear direction and purpose in our lives, we are easily bored, distracted, and tempted. Vision brings discipline and focus because we know what we're trying to accomplish. Temptations and impure desires are retrained when we have clarity because we have something positive to do with our energies.

Negative motivations are a recipe for disaster. If your motivation is to *not* be divorced, to *not* have a marriage like your parents', or to *not* commit adultery, you've more than likely set yourself up for failure. Vision is positive forward thinking which strives to accomplish the dreams you and your spouse have for your marriage.

4. Unity

Division leads to destruction. It comes from two individuals having two different visions. If there are competing visions in a marriage, then God's vision is not being lived out. Once we capture the vision for our marriages, God blesses us and pours out His provision on us so that we can be sustained. Understanding God's vision for us also unifies our marriages because we have humbly submitted ourselves to His authority. It's no longer being driven by two stubborn people trying to impose our wills on each other, which just leads to chaos and resentment.

5. Victory
Once you have stepped into the vision God has for you, you receive the prize of victory! We can't come up with good ideas to fix our marriages on our own. But when we follow God's plan, He blesses our marriages and makes us battle-ready for whatever is to come.

How to Have a Vision Retreat

1. Go alone and don't take the kids. Seeking God will not be possible with the kids along. Don't feel guilty about this. You're doing this just as much for them as you are for yourselves.

2. Put it on the calendar and make it happen. Protect this time at all costs.

3. Be patient with each other and don't get discouraged. The point is to hear from God, not to correct something you see wrong in your spouse. Don't force your spouse into this. If you're facing years of built-up toxic emotions, consider seeing a counselor before going on your retreat.

4. Seek God's will by faith and believe that He will speak to you.

5. Understand how vision happens and respect each other. God gives us vision in different ways: hearing, seeing, and feeling. If you both

receive the same vision, whether or not you received it in the same *way*, then it is from God. If you receive conflicting visions, then keep praying because it isn't from God.

6. Make a list of the things you are going to discuss in your retreat. Make sure all the important issues are discussed and prayed over thoroughly.

7. Write everything down. Remember to keep the atmosphere joyful and God-centered.

SCRIPTURE READING

Seek the LORD and His strength;
Seek His face evermore! (1 Chronicles 16:11).

When there is no vision, the people are unrestrained,
But happy is one who keeps the Law
(Proverbs 29:18 NASB).

Can two walk together, unless they are agreed?
(Amos 3:3).

If any of you lacks wisdom, let him ask of God, who gives to all liberally and without reproach, and it will be given to him. But let him ask in faith, with no doubting, for he who doubts is like a wave of the sea driven and tossed by the wind. For let not that man suppose that he will receive anything from the Lord (James 1:5–7).

DISCUSSION QUESTIONS

1. In what ways could gaining a vision from God transform a marriage?

2. What obstacles tend to prevent couples form getting away together to pray and connect? How might those logistical barriers be overcome?

3. Why can it be difficult for some personalities to approach vision retreats humbly and without predetermined agendas? How can these be addressed?

4. What risks come with one spouse feeling pressured by the other to accept their vision for their marriage? How can this be avoided?

5. How might a lack of vision contribute to impure desires or boredom in marriage? How does vision produce purity?

REFLECTION QUESTIONS

1. Why did God put you with your spouse? How can discovering that reason deepen your relationship with each other?

2. Does your marriage currently have more of your own individual visions or a shared vision from God?

3. When making important decisions, do you actively pray and seek God's will together?

4. Have you ever gone on a vision retreat with your spouse? If yes, how did it impact your marriage? If no, would you consider trying it?
5. What are some practical issues you want to discuss and pray through on a vision retreat?

CONNECT WITH GOD

Dear Father, thank You for designing marriage with Your perfect plan. Give us the vision for our lives and for our children's lives so that we can run the race well and fight the good fight of faith. Keep our minds pure and focused on You. Help us to come together in the unity of Your Spirit. Not our will, but Your will be done. May we approach this time humbly and in love for Your sake and for the sake of our family. In Jesus' name, Amen.

9

The Law of Partnership

THE BIG IDEA

In marriage, two people become one flesh by entering into a partnership by merging and sharing all
aspects of life. A lifetime of sacrifice produces an
enriching marriage.

REVIEW

According to Genesis 2:24, sexual intercourse takes
one male and one female and makes them physically
and spiritually one with each other ("one flesh").
When they become one flesh, they enter into the
Law of Partnership, which is the key to establishing
trust and intimacy in a relationship. Breaking this law
will lead to broken trust and a strained relationship.

Marriage is a complete union that places all the
things once individually owned and managed now
under both the husband and wife as a whole. Anything
that is withheld from this union produces legitimate
jealousy and division. This includes everything that

the two spouses own. The apostle Paul wrote to the Corinthians that in marriage we even give joint ownership of our bodies to our spouses. This does not give permission for sexual abuse, but it does mean that the extent of joint ownership covers everything.

What does this not mean? It does not mean you have the right to use your spouse's possessions to punish or manipulate them into doing something for your benefit. For example, just because you are both one flesh, it does not give you the right to withhold sex when they don't do things your way. That is abuse, and it will only cause your spouse to resent you and resent having sex with you. There may be times of the month when a woman's body is unavailable for intercourse, and that is legitimate. Outside of that, her body belongs to her husband, just as his body belongs to her. It is equally wrong for either a husband or a wife to withhold sex.

Trust is of major importance to the success of a marriage. If you don't trust your spouse with every area of your life, they will feel violated, just as you would feel violated if they did not trust you with every part of their life.

Finances are another area that causes tension in marriages. When a man and woman are married, their financial situations should be shared. That being said, just because it is right for one spouse to share (for example) the big inheritance they received, that does not give the other spouse the right to use it for whatever they want. *Both* people in the relationship own the money and should discuss what to do with it. Using money for the needs and desires of one spouse over the other violates trust and shows a lack of respect.

In the case of people who remarry, any children that are brought with one or both spouses are to be brought under this law of partnership as well. The biological parent should share ownership and control of the children with the nonbiological parent. If the nonbiological parent is shown that they cannot be trusted to correct and raise the children, how can they ever feel that their spouse trusts them at all? And when the children see that their biological parent doesn't fully respect their stepparent, they won't respect them either. When discipling stepchildren, it is best for the biological parent to be the enforcer, but the stepparent should be given an equal voice in the decision-making.

Did you know that you can also share your pain and past hurts? The scars from your past can negatively impact your marriage because whatever pain you feel will be felt by your spouse one way or another. You can prevent this, however, by opening up with your spouse and sharing your pain. Open every door of pain in your life. Let them have ownership of it so that they can help you heal and move forward. Some spouses don't want to receive their partner's pain. In those cases, you can still receive freedom by opening up to a spiritual leader or a Christian counselor. When you're freed from those hurts, your marriage will change for the better.

A man or woman who feels violated because their spouse won't surrender an area of their life is not being petty or unreasonable. Jesus Himself said that anyone who desires a relationship with Him but doesn't give up everything can't be His disciple (see Luke 14:33). This doesn't mean selling everything you own and joining a monastery. Jesus is saying that everything we have must be submitted to His authority. Anything that we refuse to place under His authority becomes an idol.

The same thing is true with our spouses. When we refuse to submit something to them, we're telling them that they are not as important as whatever we're holding onto and that we don't trust them. Prenuptial agreements are, in general, very dangerous because they say from the start that we aren't willing to share everything with our future spouses. The exception would be for those who have built up a sizable estate for their children and grandchildren from a previous marriage. To protect that inheritance, a prenuptial agreement is legitimate as long as there is a discussion beforehand between the man and woman coming together in order to reach a full agreement.

When you marry, you inherit the good with the bad. If you don't like your in-laws, tough. You take the good with the bad. When Your child misbehaves, you may be tempted to say to your spouse, "See what *your* child just did?" But you both have responsibility for the good and the bad.

When both spouses adhere to the law of partnership, their lives are intertwined and inseparable. Their marriage becomes sweet and intimate, just as God designed it to be. It is a union of continual selfless living that is worth every sacrifice made.

SCRIPTURE READING

And they shall become one flesh (Genesis 2:24).

"For whoever desires to save his life will lose it, but whoever loses his life for My sake will find it" (Matthew 16:25).

The husband should fulfill his marital duty to his wife, and likewise the wife to her husband. The wife does not have authority over her own body but yields it to her husband. In the same way, the husband does not have authority over his own body but yields it to his wife (1 Corinthians 7:3–4 NIV).

DISCUSSION QUESTIONS

1. What does the concept of "one flesh" mean for a marital relationship according to Genesis 2:24?

2. What role does trust play in the ability to give oneself fully to one's spouse in marriage?

3. How might refusing to merge aspects of one's life into the marriage violate the rights of the other spouse?

4. What are some examples of things that married couples often refuse to surrender to joint control? What effect does this tendency have?

5. How does God's "one flesh" design for marriage compare to society's standards of relationships today? How can Christian couples fight the temptation to conform to society?

REFLECTION QUESTIONS

1. Are you completely surrendered to your spouse? Is there something you are holding back and not sharing with them?

2. Are you controlling your spouse, or do you treat them as an equal?

3. Do you tend to say "my child" or "your child" when it comes to discipline or claiming success? How can this harm your marriage?

4. Have you allowed your spouse to accept all the good parts about you but not the more difficult aspects? How does this violate the law of partnership?

5. What might need to change in your expectations or behaviors to better align with God's design for oneness in your marriage?

CONNECT WITH GOD

Dear Father, thank You for the gift of marriage. It is a sweet, blessed union that we are grateful to be a part of. Forgive us for withholding anything from our spouses, even our joys and our hurts. Help us to open up and share whatever we've been holding back. We choose to trust our spouses, and we commit to being trustworthy for them as well. Thank You for the joy that comes when we obey the law of partnership and become one flesh. In Jesus' name, Amen.

10

Disarming Destructive Dominance

THE BIG IDEA

Dominance by either spouse destroys intimacy in a relationship. Partnership built on mutual honor and humility brings the fulfillment and blessing to a marriage that God originally designed.

REVIEW

The law of partnership is an absolute in marriage because God designed both the husband and the wife as complete equals. When one partner holds dominance over the other, intimacy is lost. Dominance is a big reason why so many people today equate marriage with pain and suffering instead of pleasure. God originally created marriage to be a pleasure and delight. In the Garden of Eden, Adam and Eve were created in unashamed intimacy as equals. However, after they rebelled against God, He cursed their relationship. Not only will the woman have increased labor pains, but she will want to control her husband (and he will dominate her instead—see Genesis 3:16). That was not God's original intention for marriage, but Adam and Eve's rebellion brought it upon mankind.

The curse is still in the world today, but through the grace of Jesus Christ, we have the law of partnership which breaks the curse off our marriages. We can live in marriage as if we're living in Eden. We will still fall short of perfection while we're on this earth, but dominance doesn't have to destroy our intimacy.

Dominance is when one partner has disproportionate control over aspects of the marriage, such as the children, finances, sex, etc. It is a gender-neutral issue, and it is wrong and damaging whether the dominant partner is the man or woman. Let's address some of the major causes of dominance.

Strong personality

Some people naturally have a Type A personality, which means they have a strong tendency to lead. Unfortunately, this is the personality that tends to want to dominate if it's been left unchecked. Dominant people also tend to be attracted to quieter and less confident people and vice versa, because they help each other emotionally. The dominant partner has someone to control, and the insecure partner has someone who will lead them. This sort of relationship never works because it goes against God's design of two *equals* living in marriage.

If you are someone with a strong personality, the key is humility in every situation. Rather than use your personality to intimidate or manipulate your spouse, use it to encourage them and find their own confidence. If you're married to someone with a strong personality, lovingly stand your ground and continue to insist that they show you respect and consideration. Most importantly of all, don't give into their intimidation tactics.

Iniquities and inner vows

Dominant behavior is usually learned from domineering parents and through generational family systems. These bad examples tend to bend people in the wrong direction. In the Old Testament, the word for *iniquity* means 'to bend or twist.' Iniquities can be passed down as generational curses. Dominance is an example of an iniquity. To be freed of it, you must repent, forgive your family for their part in passing it on to you, and submit this area of your life to Jesus. Then it will not get passed on to your children.

Inner vows also bend us in the wrong direction. Dominance is sometimes the result of having vowed something like, "No one is ever going to hurt or control me again." But Jesus tells us not to swear anything to ourselves or to others because when we do that, we are making ourselves lord over that area. If you have made any inner vows, repent and submit that area of your life completely to Jesus. He will take care of it for you.

A distorted concept of male authority

There have been cultures and time periods where is was normal for the men to dominate society, especially in marriage. That was never God's design, and it never works. God created husbands and wives to submit to each other as equals in the fear of God, with humility and love (see Ephesians 5:21–28). God's design is fulfilled when a loving and honoring husband marries a loving and honoring wife.

Pride

The Bible equates stubbornness with the sin of idolatry because it's the worship of our own opinion. Stubborn people pride themselves on *their* way of doing things and struggle to acknowledge that anyone else might be right. Pride justifies dominance because it believes that it's superior to everyone. Pride can be dealt with when we repent of our wrong thinking and pray for humility to fill our hearts instead.

Fear and insecurity

A dominating personality is usually a sign of deep-seated fear and insecurity, especially from being hurt in the past. They want to control everything because they are afraid that their fears will come true. Fear is a demonic spirit, which means we don't have to act on it, and we don't have to let it control us. We have a choice to resist it. Responding in fear makes your fears come true. Responding in faith makes your dreams come true.

SCRIPTURE READING

"Again you have heard that it was said to those of old, 'You shall not swear falsely, but shall perform your oaths to the Lord.' But I say to you, do not swear at all: neither by heaven, for it is God's throne; nor by the earth, for it is His footstool; nor by Jerusalem, for it is the city of the great King. Nor shall you swear by your head, because you cannot make one hair white or black. But let your 'Yes' be 'Yes,' and your 'No,' 'No.' For whatever is more than these is from the evil one" (Matthew 5:33–37).

> For rebellion *is as* the sin of witchcraft,
> And stubbornness *is as* iniquity and idolatry
> (1 Samuel 15:23).

For God has not given us a spirit of fear, but of power and of love and of a sound mind (2 Timothy 1:7).

DISCUSSION QUESTIONS

1. How does dominance violate God's partnership design for marriage? How can this problem be addressed?

2. What are some ways dominance may develop in a person? How can knowing this help us deal with it?

3. How did the curse in Genesis 3:16 prophesy ongoing power struggles between husbands and wives? Do you see the reality of this in the world today?

4. How can iniquities and inner vows contribute to controlling attitudes?

5. How can the principles in this chapter help transform future generations if applied to our marriages?

REFLECTION QUESTIONS

1. Have you witnessed the negative effects of dominance in your own or someone else's marriage? What was the result?

2. Are there any controlling tendencies or insecurities in your attitudes or behaviors? How can you identify them and address them?

3. What practical steps can you take to develop[mutual submission in your marital roles and decisions?

4. How can you seek to replace fear with faith and courage, especially in areas that concern your marriage?

5. What is the Holy Spirit calling you to submit to Him so that you can embrace His design for marriage?

CONNECT WITH GOD

Dear Father, we repent of our iniquities and inner vows. Forgive us for making ourselves lord over our own lives. We surrender to You and ask You to be Lord instead. We forgive our families for any part they may have had in passing down those iniquities and vows. They did not understand what they were doing. If we are dominating, teach us humility and gentleness. If we are insecure, teach us to stand up in firm but loving ways. In Jesus name, Amen.

11

Growing Together

THE BIG IDEA

Emotions and feelings can be the biggest liars in our lives. When we gauge the success of our marriages based on our emotions, we quickly get into trouble. Staying engaged as a couple purposefully and spiritually is the key to a lifetime of marital growth.

REVIEW

The most common thing distressed spouses tend to say about their failing marriages is that they've grown apart. It's always because the law of partnership is being violated somehow so that the two who became one now feel like they're two again.

Three Steps to Growing Together

1. Do not make decisions based on your emotions.
The majority of divorces do not involve high-conflict marriages. Rather, they happen because of a sudden

emotion that made it seem like the right thing to do at the time. If the couples had only decided to work on their problems and not succumbed to their feelings, they could have worked things out. A high percentage of unhappy couples who stick it out turn out to be very happy together after several years. Marital unhappiness is rarely permanent. Therefore, divorcing based on temporary negative emotions is often a mistake.

One of the devil's favorite pastimes is to remind you of the worst parts or moments of your marriage and play it on repeat in your mind. He wants to convince you that the hard times are doomed to happen again, that things will never change for the better, and that you're stuck in a prison of unhappiness. Don't take the bait. When we make rash decisions based on fleeting emotions, we're left just as miserable as we were before but with extra regret piled on top.

The Lord rewards us when we follow Him and the convictions He gives us rather than following our emotions. Emotions are not inherently evil, but they are not trustworthy. Why?

- Feelings are fickle and unpredictable.
- Feelings may be very real but very wrong.
- The devil has access to our emotions (see Ephesians 4:26–27).
- God doesn't bless emotions. He blesses obedience.

2. Build your lives and the purpose of your lives together.

When God created Adam and Eve, He blessed them as a couple, not as individuals. He designed their marriage to be a union of their hearts and purposes. Anyone who wants to live an independent and selfish life should not get married. Marriage means building your life together with someone else and becoming one flesh with them.

Couples grow apart because they are already apart. They're living separate lives because they'd rather do what they want and just have their husband or wife as an accessory. Just because a couple is married and living together doesn't mean that they will automatically feel close to each other. If things outside of the marriage are their priority, then they won't need their spouse and children. There's no purpose for why they're together. That leads to misery and divorce.

What is the reason God put you together? Once you figure that out, you can work to build your marriage, and you'll grow together for the rest of your lives.

3. Grow in your relationship with the Lord and your local church.

Because marriage was created by God, it is as much a spiritual relationship as it is a physical one (and maybe even more so). Therefore, marriage is governed by spiritual laws, and marital love is based on a spiritual love.

We don't naturally possess the ability to love. Because we live in a fallen world and have sinful flesh, we can't love the way God designed us to love. The world's love is weak, fickle, and often misguided. But God *is* love (see 1 John 4:8), and He is able to empower us by His Holy Spirit to show strong, dependable love. We desperately need Him in us in order to have strong relationships and strong marriages. Without the Holy Spirit, we're like engines with no oil in them. We can't function properly, and eventually we break down. The Holy Spirit keeps us moving. With Him at the helm, our lives and marriages only get better and better!

Spending time with the Lord on our own and together with our spouses is crucial. This is the time when we cast all our cares on the Lord (see 1 Peter 5:7) and allow the Spirit to fill us with His power.

There are so many forces in the world that are determined to tear apart our marriages. But the power of the Holy Spirit is stronger than any of those forces. That's why it's so important to commit to seeking the Lord and to staying in community with a Bible-believing church and fellow believers. To overcome the evil in this world, we need support. We need to be in an army to fight the good fight of faith. Couples who drop out of church tend to see serious problems arise in their marriages before long. When we go to church or have fellowship with other believers, we're equipped with the right armor and weapons, and our marriages grow stronger.

SCRIPTURE READING

"Be angry, and do not sin": do not let the sun go down on your wrath, nor give place to the devil (Ephesians 4:26–27).

Then God blessed them, and God said to them, "Be fruitful and multiply; fill the earth and subdue it; have dominion over the fish of the sea, over the birds of the air, and over every living thing that moves on the earth" (Genesis 1:28).

And the LORD God said, "*It is* not good that man should be alone; I will make him a helper comparable to him" (Genesis 2:18).

But the fruit of the Spirit is love, joy, peace, long-suffering, kindness, goodness, faithfulness, gentleness, self-control. Against such there is no law (Galatians 5:22–23).

DISCUSSION QUESTIONS

1. Why do the majority of divorces not actually involve high-conflict marriages? What other factors lead couples to divorce?

2. In what ways can feelings be unreliable guides for decision-making in marriage? What are some examples? How does relying on the Holy Spirit differ?

3. How might harboring anger or bitterness open the door for the enemy? What can this lead to?

4. Why can't marriage be sustained as a private affair? What support do couples need?

5. What patterns occur when couples disconnect from regular church participation? What tends to happen as a result?

REFLECTION QUESTIONS

1. Have you ever felt yourself "growing apart" from your spouse? What was happening during that time that might have caused it?

2. Do you tend to make decisions based on short-term circumstances or emotions rather than taking the long view? What might need to shift?

3. To what extent have you built your life's purpose together with your spouse? In what areas are you still operating independently?

4. How consistently do you rely on the Spirit's power to love your spouse? Are you often tempted to depend on your own feelings and willpower instead?

5. Would you say there is true emotional intimacy in your marriage right now? If no, what is getting in the way?

CONNECT WITH GOD

Dear Father, we don't want to be led by our fickle emotions, so we submit them to You today and ask You to lead us as our Lord and King. Teach us to hear Your voice no matter what our feelings may be. Holy Spirit, fill us with Your fruit of love, joy, and peace. Dwell in us so that we can demonstrate Your kind, perfect nature to the rest of the world and especially to our spouses. My we grow closer together with our spouses and with You every day. In Jesus' name, Amen.

12

Financial Intimacy and Partnership

THE BIG IDEA

Money issues are one of the most common causes of divorce. God intends for married couples to be blessed financially, and pursuing true financial partnership, rather than selfish control, is the key to unlocking that blessing.

REVIEW

Money is an essential part of everyday life. When we join together in marriage, we are forced to make financial decisions together. Refusing to reach a mutual agreement concerning money will place unnecessary stress on the relationship. It is always best that a husband and wife work together as financial partners.

4 Steps to Building Financial Intimacy and Partnership

1. Mutual Respect

There are four financial personality types or money languages:

- Driver: Money means success. It wards off incompetence.
- Analytic: Money means security. It wards off chaos/loss of control.
- Amiable: Money means love. It wards off loss of affection/relationship.
- Expressive: Money means acceptance. It wards off rejection.

This is important to keep in mind because it helps couples understand why their spouse uses or saves money the way they do. God created us to see money in different ways so that spouses can balance each other out with their respective strengths. In fact, you're better off if your spouse has a different financial personality than you. If you both speak the same money language, it would be a good idea to get financial counseling so that someone can provide balance and perspective.

2. Shared Control

The law of partnership requires that everything brought into the marriage by both spouses is now jointly owned. It doesn't matter what it is. If one or both spouses withhold something, they provoke their spouse to legitimate jealousy. It's not just a matter of owning it legally. By God's law, those items (especially money) belong to both partners *spiritually* as well.

It doesn't matter who in the relationship has more expertise with money. It doesn't matter who's in charge of writing the checks or managing the budget. You are equals. Neither spouse has the right to exert control over the finances or the financial information. Both partners have the right to know their financial situation at all times. There is no legitimate reason to withhold it from one another. Every decision should be made together.

3. Proactive Planning

There are three descending levels of financial decision-making:

- Proactive decision-making: making decisions in advance.
- Reactive decision-making: constantly reacting to financial issues and pressures you haven't talked about.
- Radioactive decision-making: certain financial issues become too dangerous to discuss because your emotions are too high.

Every couple needs to sit down proactively and make a detailed budget of their finances. If you feel you can't do it on your own, go to a financial counselor for help. A budget helps you make decisions in advance so that you're not under constant pressure and anxiety when it comes to your finances. It keeps you both accountable to spend your money wisely and ranks your family's priorities. Without it, emotions become tense because life is less certain. It becomes even worse if you fall into debt.

4. Shared Faith

Submit your finances to God. When you have a decision to make, pray about it until you are both in agreement and have peace about it (see Colossians 3:15). God wants to guide you and give you tangible peace in your life. Making decisions based on your feelings and understanding can be dangerous. A situation may seem perfect, but if God does not give you peace about it, there is something potentially harmful that you can't see.

If you don't pray, you're going to worry. Worse, you won't get God's direction. He is your Father, and He loves you. He wants to bring you to the very best He has in store for you. He will guide you and your spouse through a shared sense of peace.

A crucial part of shared faith is tithing (giving the first 10 percent) of our finances to the Lord.

Perhaps you won't see a change immediately, but tithing shows two things: that you trust the Lord, as Maker of the universe, to provide for your every need and that you understand that everything you own belongs to Him. When you give in faith, the Lord is always faithful to provide for you and cause you to see increase. This is the only area where we are allowed to test God (see Malachi 3:10), and He will pass the test every time.

SCRIPTURE READING

And let the peace of God rule in your hearts, to which also you were called in one body; and be thankful (Colossians 3:15).

"Bring all the tithes into the storehouse,
That there may be food in My house,
And try Me now in this,"
Says the LORD of hosts,
"If I will not open for you the windows of heaven
And pour out for you *such* blessing
That *there will* not *be room* enough *to receive it*" (Malachi 3:10).

DISCUSSION QUESTIONS

1. Why should nothing in marriage be individually owned or controlled? What happens when one spouse tries to control or hide financial information from the other?

2. What problems may arise from both spouses having the same financial personality/money language? How can differing viewpoints lead to better decision making?

3. How does sharing control of the finances improve intimacy? Why is the person with more financial expertise not justified in controlling everything? What sorts of behaviors violate the law of partnership?

4. How does proactive financial planning through the use of a budget improve marital harmony and intimacy? How can debt negatively impact relationships?

5. How can Colossians 3:15 provide guidance for how to make decisions? Why is it better to rely on this than trying to figure everything out ourselves?

REFLECTION QUESTIONS

1. Can you identify your own money language? Your spouse's money language? How could understanding each other's languages help prevent arguments about finances?

2. Do you agree that having different financial personalities can be an advantage in marriage if respected? Why or why not?

3. Have you experienced God's blessing through tithing? If not, what beliefs may be holding you back from testing His promise?

4. How has this chapter expanded or challenged your perspectives on money and intimacy? What existing assumptions or habits might need re-evaluation?

5. Has conflict over finances been a problem in your marriage? If so, how? What practical steps can you and your spouse take to restore harmony and intimacy?

CONNECT WITH GOD

Dear Father, we submit our families' finances to You. Teach us to be understanding and accept our spouses' differences, especially when it comes to money. Help us to have humility and to trust our spouses with this shared responsibility that You have given us. Most of all, let us get to know You even more so that we can learn to trust that You will take care of us and provide for us even when it seems impossible. In Jesus' name, Amen.

13

The Law of Purity

THE BIG IDEA

Adam and Eve had the perfect marriage before the Fall, but sin damaged their intimate relationship. As purity is restored, couples can once again be naked emotionally, spiritually, and physically without shame, enjoying marriage as God intended.

REVIEW

Before Adam and Eve ate the forbidden fruit, their genitals were shamelessly uncovered. They had no need for artificial coverings because God's perfect will was for them to be naked physically, mentally, emotionally, and spiritually. This signifies that their differences could be openly expressed (genitals are the most obvious difference); they could have unhindered intimacy; and their most sensitive areas could be exposed without fear.

We were created to be completely exposed to our spouses. Aside from our relationship with God, there is no other relationship in life that affords the potential for as much "nakedness" as marriage. It is necessary in marriage that spouses are naked before each other in every way. This can only occur in an atmosphere of honesty and vulnerability.

After Adam and Eve ate the forbidden fruit, sin entered the relationship, and they had to cover themselves. This led to three changes: differences cannot be safely expressed where sin is present; sin damages and often destroys the atmosphere necessary to breed intimacy; and the sensitive areas of our lives and delicate issues in our relationships cannot be safely exposed where sin is present.

The Bible does not tell us that Adam and Eve were naked simply to reveal their nudity. It shows the original purity of mankind and marriage. Here's the root of the matter:

- Sin is always deadly. Its penalty is death no matter what kind of sin it is. Violating our spouses and harming the relationship is just as bad as any other sin.

- Purity must be upheld by both partners in order for the relationship to provide a climate for total exposure. There's no such thing as "private sin." One spouse's sin *will* affect the other spouse.

- Purity is for every area of marriage. The devil only needs one weak point in your life to taint you with sin, whether that's your sex life, finances, the words of your mouth, addictions, wrong priorities, selfishness, dominance, or something else.

Sin may seem fun at the time, but it only produces temporary pleasure. It's sneaky too. It kills you slowly rather than all at once. Believe it or not, purity is much more fun and will result in the best sex and intimacy you could possibly imagine for your marriage!

Seven Steps to Purity in Marriage

1. Take Responsibility for Your Own Behavior.
Whatever sin you think your spouse may be committing is less important for you to focus on compared to your own behavior. You can't change your spouse, but you can allow God to change your behavior. When you focus on letting God transform you, you're putting your spouse's behavior into the Lord's hands. He is faithful to work in their life once you remove your hands from the wheel.

2. Do Not Return Sin for Sin.
No matter what people do to us, God instructs us to return evil with good and to love even our enemies (see Luke 6:27–36). Naturally, this doesn't mean you

should allow your spouse to abuse you, but it does mean that your pure love and gentleness can be the difference in your spouse's life.

3. Admit Your Faults.

The sincerest, most heartfelt apology can bring quick healing to a broken marriage. A marriage suffers when one or both spouses refuse to admit their faults and ask for forgiveness. God forgives our sins when we bring them to Him because Jesus paid the price for our sins at the cross. But we must let Him deal with them. When we are honest about our faults with our spouses, we demonstrate vulnerability, and we show our spouses that we care for our marriages.

4. Forgive.

On the other hand, when our spouses come to us with their faults, it is important to show them the forgiveness that we desire to receive from them. Again, our heavenly Father is merciful to forgive our sins. We should be willing to do the same and bless those who hurt us. Otherwise, we will store bitterness in our hearts, which will poison the intimacy of our marriages. Once you forgive someone, make sure the hurt stays in the past.

5. Speak the Truth in Love.

When your spouse does something that hurts or annoys you, don't wait to confront them until you're angry. Go to them as soon as possible and talk through the issue in a loving way.

6. Pray for Each Other.
Nothing you say or do will ultimately change your spouse's behavior. You can't manipulate or intimidate them into straightening up. The best thing you can do is pray for them and hand them over to the Lord.

7. Seek Healthy Friends and Fellowship.
Your friends will always influence you for better or for worse. They can tempt you to sin or encourage you to seek God. It is important to run with the second crowd. There's enough temptation in the world as it is without having bad friends that will lead you down the wrong paths.

SCRIPTURE READING

And they were both naked, the man and his wife, and were not ashamed (Genesis 2:25).

"Blessed *are* the pure in heart,
For they shall see God" (Matthew 5:8).

For the wages of sin *is* death, but the gift of God *is* eternal life in Christ Jesus our Lord (Romans 6:23).

"And why do you look at the speck in your brother's eye, but do not perceive the plank in your own eye? Or how can you say to your brother, 'Brother, let me remove the speck that *is* in your eye,' when you yourself do not see the plank that *is* in your own eye? Hypocrite! First remove the plank from your own eye, and then you will see clearly to remove the speck that is in your brother's eye" (Luke 6:41–42).

> As far as the east is from the west,
> *So* far has He removed our transgressions from us (Psalm 103:12).

DISCUSSION QUESTIONS

1. How did sin affect Adam and Eve's relationship? What changed emotionally, physically, and spiritually?

2. Why is sin damaging in any relationship? What deadly effects does it have? Why is there no such thing as private sin?

3. What must both spouses do for purity to exist in marriage? Why is purity important for every area of marriage?

4. When we refuse to forgive others, God does not forgive our sins. What effects does unforgiveness have on a marriage?

5. What areas of "nakedness" did God intend for marriage? What must happen first before this kind of vulnerability can occur?

REFLECTION QUESTIONS

1. Are there areas of impurity you are harboring privately that may be hurting your marriage? How can you stand "naked" before your spouse and before God?

2. Do you retaliate or harbor unforgiveness when your spouse sins? Do you avoid the uncomfortable issues for as long as possible? How is that damaging your intimacy?

3. How well do you control your anger when talking with your spouse about problems that have come up? Do you speak harshly or with patience and love?

4. Have you surrounded yourself with pure or impure friendships? Which ones encourage your marriage and which ones harm it?

5. Which areas of your life and relationship do you need to make "naked" before your spouse?

CONNECT WITH GOD

Dear Father, we ask You to create pure hearts in us. We want our marriages to glorify You. Please forgive us of our sins and help to us to forgive our spouses' sins in the same way. We believe our marriages will be much more intimate and blessed when we submit to Your law of purity. Thank You that You have made us the righteousness of God in Christ. In Jesus' name, Amen.

14

Disarming Anger and Resolving Conflicts

THE BIG IDEA

Anger is normal, and it must be processed correctly, expressed lovingly, and resolved quickly. Unresolved anger allows the devil to influence our thoughts about our spouse, but dealing with anger quickly keeps your heart and marriage pure.

REVIEW

Even in the most intimate and peaceful marriage, it is possible to still get angry. That's not a bad thing as long as you process your anger and resolve it before it gets out of control. Acting on your anger, whether that's by shouting at your spouse or giving them the silent treatment, quickly leads to problems.

Four "Don'ts" of Anger (see Ephesians 4:26–27)

1. Don't deny your anger.
The apostle Paul makes it clear that anger is not a sin. There is nothing wrong with it. Even God gets angry. It is actually more dangerous to internalize anger than to be angry. Internalizing anger can affect you physically, emotionally, mentally, and even relationally. It won't go away until you deal with it.

To make it go away, you have to admit to your anger, just as you should allow others to admit their anger to you. The best marriages happen when you are able to be honest with each other without fear. Remember that our anger is not always valid, which is why we must show grace to each other and bring our anger to our spouses with humility.

2. Don't sin or justify bad behavior.
We are allowed to be angry, but we should never allow that anger to manifest itself as sin. We are not justified in behaving badly just because our spouses behave badly. Again, the only way to defeat a spirit is with the opposite spirit.

3. Don't go to bed on your anger.
The anger we feel today is manageable. The anger we still carry from yesterday is toxic because it has buried itself into our hearts and has been added to

any anger we feel today. This is why Paul exhorts us not to go to bed angry. If you can't resolve the issue yourselves, go to counseling until it's resolved.

4. Don't give the devil a place in your marriage.
When we go to bed angry, we open a door for the devil. The word *devil* in Greek means

'slanderer.' By going to bed angry, we allow the devil to slander our spouses to us. The enemy is subtle. We rarely realize that the bitter thoughts going through our minds are from the enemy. The devil hates your marriage and everything it represents. He will do everything he can to manipulate you into destroying your own marriage.

When we deal with our anger and marital conflicts, we are also training our children how to deal with issues in their future marriages. Remember, you're not a prisoner of your past. If your parents didn't provide you with good examples, you are not doomed to repeat their mistakes. You simply need to learn how to resolve conflict.

Four Steps for Conflict Resolution

1. Confront in a loving and positive manner.
Both spouses should be free to share their anger. Sharing anger doesn't mean screaming threats or cursing. It's going to each other in a gentle, loving way to express your feelings and to talk through the

problems together. Begin with soft, affirming words. If you lose control of your emotions, take time to get them under control. Ask the Lord to help you.

2. Complain and don't criticize.
There's a difference. Complaining is helpful and constructive. Criticism is negative and destructive. Complaining focuses on you and what might have hurt you. Criticism focuses on your spouse and what they've done wrong. Complaining asks your spouse to sit down and have a conversation about how to solve the issue. Criticism jumps to conclusions and accuses without receiving any input from the person you're accusing.

3. Listen to your spouse and believe them.
If you've spent a long period of time going to bed angry, your thoughts have been skewed and twisted. The anger that you felt has been corrupted into bitterness, and the offense against you has likely been inflated. When you sit down to talk with your spouse about what has angered you, give them the opportunity to speak too. Don't make them feel that they are guilty until proven innocent. Hear them out. That will encourage them to be open and honest with you.

4. Forgive and let it go.

We are human. All of us make mistakes. Jesus is patient with us and tenderly cleanses us with His Word. We are to follow His example in our relationships. Just like Jesus forgives you more times than you can count, you will have to be patient with your spouse and forgive them over and over and over. When you resolve conflict with your spouse, you both need to sincerely say that you forgive each other. Once you forgive each other, keep it that way. Don't drag the issue back up again after you promise to forgive them. If your spouse doesn't want to sit down and resolve the issue, you don't have to go to bed angry. Before you go to sleep, confess your anger to the Lord, then tell Him that you forgive your spouse. The Holy Spirit is the enforcer of truth, not you. You can't change them, but He can.

SCRIPTURE READING

"Be angry, and do not sin": do not let the sun go down on your wrath, nor give place to the devil (Ephesians 4:26–27).

A soft answer turns away wrath,
But a harsh word stirs up anger (Proverbs 15:1).

Love suffers long *and* is kind; love does not envy; love does not parade itself, is not puffed up; does not behave rudely, does not seek its own, is not provoked, thinks no evil; does not rejoice in iniquity, but rejoices in the truth; bears all things, believes all things, hopes all things, endures all things (1 Corinthians 13:4–7).

DISCUSSION QUESTIONS

1. What does the Bible say about anger? What danger comes with unresolved anger? Why is it important to resolve anger before going to bed?

2. Why is it important for spouses to allow each other to bring their complaints? What makes a complaint different than criticism? How should spouses listen and respond to complaints?

3. What role does the devil play concerning unresolved anger? How does he influence spouses? How can spouses prevent him from gaining a foothold?

4. Whose job is it to convict and change spouses? What happens if spouses try to take on this role? How does trusting God to work change one's attitudes and behaviors?

5. How is the law of purity upheld in marriage even in times of conflict? How do selflessness and sacrifice play into this?

REFLECTION QUESTIONS

1. Do you currently go to bed angry at your spouse? How do you think this has impacted your thoughts and feelings towards them?

2. Are there times you keep a record of wrongs done to you instead of freely forgiving? What can help you choose forgiveness, even if your spouse is unrepentant?

3. Are there any unhealthy conflict resolution patterns from your family of origin that still have an influence over you? What new patterns would you like God to help you to establish in your marriage?

4. How can remembering Jesus' patient and forgiving example empower us to resolve conflict? What first steps can you take to choose forgiveness over harboring anger?

5. Do you try to be the Holy Spirit in your relationship by trying to change your spouse? How would it impact your marriage if you stepped back into a trusting and prayerful posture?

CONNECT WITH GOD

Dear Father, if there is any bitterness in us, we release it to You. We repent of the anger we've been harboring that created that bitterness. Give us the strength and humility to admit our mistakes to our spouses. Teach us how to process our anger so that it doesn't become worse and cause us to behave in a way that we will regret. We want to love our spouses and treat them as You treat us—with gentleness and patience. Thank You for Your grace and love. In Jesus' name, Amen.

15

Everyday Intimacy

THE BIG IDEA

Intimacy in marriage consists of four dimensions: spiritual, emotional, mental, and physical. Achieving intimacy requires open sharing and connection in each of these areas. Pursuing intimacy is essential for a fulfilling marriage according to God's design.

REVIEW

No one wants to be in a passionless relationship with no sense of closeness. The dream we all have is to be married to our lover and best friend. That dream can come true if we will just understand the truth about intimacy and put it into practice.

Four Lies of Intimacy

1. Sex is intimacy.
The biggest lie people believe about intimacy is that it only improves the more sex you have. But it is

only part of it. On its own, sex hardly fulfilling. Of course, we have physical needs, but God designed us to be more than just physically driven beings. Sleeping around is promoted as something that will make you happier, but it actually only makes you empty and depressed because that's not what you were created for.

2. Intimacy is automatic when you marry the right person.
This can also be called "the soul mate myth." There is no one who is inherently more inclined to bring you intimacy, no matter how compatible you may be with each other. A marriage is successful when the husband and wife are both deliberately working together and when they honor God's design for marriage. If the couple believes that intimacy comes naturally when you marry the right person, their marriage is doomed from the start. The moment problems arise and intimacy diminishes, the devil can come to you and make you believe that your spouse isn't really the right one for you.

3. Intimacy is for certain types of people but not for everyone.
God is love, and He created us to love and receive love in return. In marriage, we experience love (both giving and receiving it) on the deepest, most satisfying level possible. Both men and women need

intimacy and love. It's not that some people need it more than others, though the way in which they give and receive love may be different.

4. Once a certain amount of damage has been done in a marriage, it is impossible to restore the intimacy.

Nothing is impossible with God. The Bible shows testimony after testimony of how God did impossible things. Since He is the same yesterday, today, and forever, we can expect Him to still do impossible things today. People rarely mess up their marriages intentionally. They just don't know any better. Marriage isn't exactly taught at the university level. Both partners in a marriage will make mistakes. That doesn't mean that the marriage is doomed. When we put our trust in Jesus, we activate our faith that God will restore our marriages and intimacy. He can do it! And He is willing.

In Mark 12:29–30, Jesus quotes Deuteronomy, which lays out the different levels of love with which we are to love God: heart, soul, mind, and strength. These levels also apply for the intimate love experienced by a married couple:

Spiritual Intimacy

Jesus says we are to love God, first, with all our hearts. Our hearts are the spiritual dimension where

He resides with us. When Adam and Eve sinned, the human race died spiritually. Through Jesus and the Holy Spirit, God forgives us of our sins, and our spirits are revived. When we believe in our hearts and confess with our mouths that Jesus is Lord, we are "born again" (see Romans 10:8–10). We receive salvation.

When we come together with our spouses to seek the Lord, inviting Him into our relationship, we experience the deepest level of intimacy possible—spiritual intimacy. When you pray, God gives you peace about the things that made you worried or irritable. We can choose whether or not we're anxious. We may not be able to stop the anxious thoughts from entering our minds, but we can decide to take those anxieties directly to the throne of God and lay them at His feet in exchange for peace. Doing that as a couple binds us and even improves our sex lives.

Emotional Intimacy

Jesus tells us to love God with all our souls. Your soul is the seat of your will and emotions. Adam and Eve were able to share their emotions with each other before the Fall. That is the type of emotional intimacy we are meant to have today. Your true "soul mate" is the husband or wife you choose to open up to emotionally and share your soul with. This is done through loving honesty and allowing feelings to be shared without judgment or rejection.

Mental Intimacy

Jesus says to love God with all our minds, which means using our brains to think about Him, know Him, seek Him, and worship Him. In the same way, loving our spouse with our minds means we think about them, study them to know them better, and focus on them. We learn about each other by regularly sharing our thoughts. We should never share our thoughts in a hurtful way, but it is important to talk about the things that can be improved.

Physical Intimacy

This is not just about having sex. Even outside of the bedroom, we need to be physically affectionate people. Both men and women need nonsexual affection. It's also important for our children to witness it so that they know that their parents love each other. This way, they also see how they are to treat their future spouses.

SCRIPTURE READING

> Then Jesus said, "Father, forgive them, for they do not know what they do" (Luke 23:34).

> And because you are sons, God has sent forth the Spirit of His Son into your hearts, crying out, "Abba, Father!" (Galatians 4:6).

Jesus answered him, "The first of all the command-
ments *is*: 'Hear, O Israel, the LORD our God, the
LORD is one. And you shall love the LORD your
God with all you heart, with all your soul, with all
your mind, and with all your strength.' This *is* the
first commandment" (Mark 12:29–30).

DISCUSSION QUESTIONS

1. What was intimacy like in Eden before the
   Fall? How has sin corrupted marital intimacy
   for most couples? What can we learn from
   how God's original design?

2. What are some benefits of a couple praying
   together regularly? How can inviting God into
   a marriage affect intimacy?

3. What allows for emotional intimacy to grow
   between spouses? How can understanding each other's differences lead to deeper
   intimacy?

4. How can couples achieve mental intimacy?
   Why is honesty and freely sharing thoughts
   important for this aspect?

5. Beyond sex, what does physical intimacy
   require? Why are these other aspects important? What impact can a couple's intimacy
   have on children in the home?

REFLECTION QUESTIONS

1. Which of the four lies about intimacy have you most believed or heard others claim? Why do these lies persist? How can we combat them?

2. Do you create space for emotional intimacy by freely sharing feelings without judgment? Are there any barriers that make this hard to achieve?

3. Would you describe your marriage as having strong mental intimacy where you openly communicate your thoughts to your spouse? Why or why not?

4. Beyond sex, do you and your spouse regularly show each other nonsexual affection? How might you improve in this area?

5. Which area of intimacy is most lacking in your marriage currently? What practical steps can you take to improve intimacy in that dimension?

CONNECT WITH GOD

Dear Father, thank You for Your love. We could not have loved You without You first loving us. We want to have deeper intimacy with You, just as we want to have deeper intimacy with our spouses. As we pursue You together, help us to strengthen our relationship.

Show us where we may be lacking intimacy or giving a bad example to our children. Help us to grow closer together. Give us the courage to open up to each other. In Jesus' name, Amen.

16

True Sexual Intimacy

THE BIG IDEA

Our society is sexually confused, and it is damaging the intimacy of our marriages. The only way to have true sexual intimacy is to view sex in a biblical, covenantal manner. God should always be the center of the marriage, and sex is the sacred seal.

REVIEW

The primary reason why so marriages in our society today lack intimacy is because there is an excess of ways to experience sexual stimulation and excitement (the most prevalent of which is pornography). Statistics show that Christians—both men and women—are just as trapped as the rest of society.

Sexual intimacy is only one-fourth of where we experience true intimacy in marriage, and even then, nonsexual affection is just as important. An overdependence on sex results in divorces, sexual addictions, and sexual isolation. So many people prefer to have self-stimulated sexual experiences over the real thing. But God created us to bond to only one person. Sex releases a series of hormones that reduce stress and help us bond with our spouses.

When we participate in any sexual activity not with our spouses, the chemicals are so strong that they confuse our brains into attaching to someone other than our spouses. That is why the mind is the most powerful sex organ we have.

Couples who watch porn to get sexually stimulated before having sex are inviting others into their bedrooms. Rather than increasing intimacy, it diminishes it. We're saying that our spouses aren't enough for us and don't give us enough pleasure.

Sex is a spiritual experience. The reason secular society lacks intimacy is because it fails to recognize this. God created sex for marriage. When we have sex with someone, we become permanently, spiritually connected.

If you used to have casual sex in the past and created many soul ties, there is hope for you that those ties can be broken. Repent of sexual immorality to God and then pray that those ties are broken in Jesus' name. Once those are broken, remove all reminders of the people involved with those ties and break off contact with them. If you are addicted to pornography, confess your problem to God and to someone who can help keep you accountable.

For true sexual intimacy, we must understand that marriage is a covenant. The Hebrew word for *covenant* means 'to cut,' which means blood is spilled. A covenant relationship is a sacrificial and permanent relationship, and it requires a high price. It is a sacred relationship with God at the center. Casual sex is not covenant sex. On the other hand, marital sex is the seal and sign that consummates the wedding vows.

Practical Steps to Sexual pleasure and Intimacy In Marriage

1. Pray and invite God into your sexuality.
Maybe it sounds uncomfortable, but there is nothing weird about having God at the center of your sexuality. It isn't gross to Him; He created it! Trust Him to increase your sexual desire. There is nothing you can hide from Him. He is a safe place, a compassionate healer, and a loving Father.

2. Have a vision for your sex life.
Just as it's important to talk about the vision of your marriage, it is also important to get a vision for your sex life together before you get into bed. Share your

sexual likes and dislikes. Figure out how to please each other.

3. Be a sexual servant to your spouse.

The servant spirit should permeate your marriage, even the bedroom. When your desire is to please each other, especially sexually, sex becomes the most amazing experience. Nothing kills intimacy like selfishness.

4. Take turns being the focus of the experience.

God designed us all with different sexual natures and needs. With this in mind, one way to serve each other is to spend one night focusing on "his needs" and the next focusing on "her needs." Both types of needs are equally important to fulfill, and it will create a beautiful win-win experience.

5. Be adventurous and creative.

This does not mean you always have to be coming up with something new. But it is just as problematic to always be changing and experimenting as it is to get into a rut and do sex one way all the time. Regarding sex toys, the biggest questions should always be "Is it safe?" and "Does it harm our relationship?" The important thing is to remember that sex has many reasons, including reproduction, comfort, sensual enjoyment and pleasure, bonding, and as a covenant sign of good faith.

6. Be romantic in your spouse's language all day long.

Sex really begins the moment you wake up. If you're sensitive to your spouse and show them spiritual, mental, and emotional intimacy throughout the day, your sex life will be all the more fulfilling.

7. Never give up.

Whatever problems arise, deal with them at once. The things that affect you will also affect your spouse one way or another. Your marriage is too important and too sacred to let anything mess with it. Maintain the intimacy of sex. God's design is perfect, and His plans for you are worth it. Fight for your marriage! Let your spouse know that you're committed to fighting for your marriage. You and your spouse will see your marriage and intimacy grow stronger and stronger.

SCRIPTURE READING

Do you not know that your bodies are members of Christ? Shall I then take the members of Christ and make *them* members of a harlot? Certainly not! Or do you not know that he who is joined to a harlot is one body *with her?* For "the two," He says, "shall become one flesh." But he who is joined to the Lord is one spirit *with Him.*

Flee sexual immorality. Every sin that a man does is outside the body, but he who commits sexual immorality sins against his own body. Or do you not know that your body is the temple of the Holy Spirit *who is* in you, whom you have from God, and you are not your own? For you were bought at a price; therefore glorify God in your body and in your spirit, which are God's (1 Corinthians 6:15–20).

Marriage *is* honorable among all, and the bed undefiled; but fornicators and adulterers God will judge (Hebrews 13:4).

DISCUSSION QUESTIONS

1. How has technology impacted sexual excitement and intimacy? Why doesn't this increase in sexual stimulation improve marriages?

2. What is the spiritual nature of sex? What happens spiritually when pornography is viewed? What are "soul ties," and how are they created and broken?

3. Why is it important to emphasize sex as a God-centered covenant? What does the word *covenant* mean, and why is that important?

4. How should couples deal with differing sexual natures and needs? Why is it important to understand the multidimensional reasons for sex?

5. Why is it important to meet emotional needs and have all-day romance? What happens when emotional intimacy needs are ignored?

REFLECTION QUESTIONS

1. How have technology and the media impacted your own views of sex and intimacy in relationships? What ideas have harmed your understanding?

2. Have you considered the concept of "soul ties" before? How might they have impacted your sexual history or views?

3. Do you currently view your marriage as a covenant with God at the center? Would a shift to this perspective strengthen your relationship?

4. Do you feel your differing sexual needs are balanced well, or could designating "his night" and "her night" be helpful to you?

5. What specific ideas from this chapter would be most helpful for strengthening intimacy in your own marriage? How might you apply them?

CONNECT WITH GOD

Dear Father, thank You for teaching us about sacrificial love. In Your love and by Your blood, cleanse us of all our sins. We want to do what is most honoring to You. We want our marriages to be for Your glory. Keep us selfless and gentle. Let us demonstrate the fruits of Your Spirit. Thank You for the incredible gift of intimacy and for the beautiful covenant seal of sex. Deepen our love for our spouses more and more. In Jesus' name, Amen.